ACCOUNTING

FINANCIAL ACCOUNTING

HOW TO STUDY ACCOUNTING
Janet Cassagio
Nassau Community College

ACCOUNTING
SECOND EDITION

FINANCIAL
ACCOUNTING

Charles T. Horngren
Stanford University

Walter T. Harrison, Jr.
Baylor University

MATH REVIEW
William Harvey
Henry Ford Community College

Prentice Hall
Englewood Cliffs, New Jersey 07632

© 1990 by **PRENTICE-HALL, INC.**
A Simon & Schuster Company
Englewood Cliffs, N.J. 07632

10   9   8   7   6   5

ISBN 0-13-400870-7

Printed in the United States of America

CONTENTS

HOW TO STUDY ACCOUNTING   1

MATH REVIEW   10

ACCOUNTING

FINANCIAL
ACCOUNTING

HOW TO STUDY ACCOUNTING

INTRODUCTION

How to study accounting is often only the second question on a student's mind. The first question is why.

A knowledge of accounting helps us to make the most advantageous decisions about our personal finances. Savings accounts, checking accounts, car payments, credit cards, loans, taxes, investments—these are some typical financial concerns that are based on accounting.

In most businesses, a knowledge of accounting is an essential element of a successful career. Surveys conducted by respected business publications show that managers value an accounting background. A striking proportion of employees in the higher and more responsible positions, including heads of major corporations, are educated in accounting.

A Cumulative Study

Accounting is not a mystery. It is a tool that people developed to fill a need— the need to keep track of what we own.

If there is a secret to learning accounting, it is that accounting is a cumulative discipline. Each successive topic that you learn relies heavily on what you have learned before. Your textbook (*Accounting*, by Horngren and Harrison) is organized so that you learn the most fundamental concepts and procedures first, and continue to build on them. Your accounting professor also will begin with the simplest material and continuously add to it in greater depth and detail.

To learn accounting, you must master the earlier chapters, particularly the first five, which describe the accounting cycle. This knowledge is your basis for further study.

Studying Accounting Effectively

When students run into difficulty, it is generally because they have either forgotten the earlier material or have not learned it well enough to move forward. This booklet will help you find ways to study accounting more effectively and improve you ability to master the material.

Some of the suggestions may seem obvious. These are included primarily to serve as a reminder. In many places, alternative choices have been included so that you can decide which suggestion suits your needs or habits best. As you read, note the options that are most appropriate to your personality. You may also want to consider trying some that seem inappropriate as well—you may be pleasantly surprised to find that these work for you.

Planning Your Approach

This booklet is divided into two main sections: 1) Classwork, and 2) Homework and Study Habits. Each of these sections has two subdivisions—one for the steps that are essential to mastering this course, the other for suggestions from which you can choose the ones you find most helpful.

All references to the text are to *Accounting* by Horngren and Harrison, Prentice Hall, 1989.

Remember, we all must learn to accept responsibility for our own success or failure in a given subject or situation. We earn our own results; no one "gives" us anything. Consider this carefully as you plan your approach to learning your coursework.

CLASSWORK: THE ESSENTIALS

These are things you must do in order to learn the material and do well in your accounting course.

Maintain a good attendance record.   This is essential not only for continuity, but also to hear which topics or concepts your professor emphasizes and which ones are considered less important. Copying notes from other classmates may not always show you the proper emphasis.

Participate actively in the class.   If you are allowed to choose your own seat, make sure you choose one where can hear and be heard. Don't be afraid to ask or respond to questions. Try to overcome fear, shyness, or a lack of confidence. Commit yourself to ask or answer just one question; it may lead to more. Remember, if you have a question, someone else in the class is probably wondering about the same thing.

Do not use memorization as a substitute for understanding. You need to understand both the reasons and the mechanics of accounting. There are definitions and procedures that you will have to memorize, but be sure you understand them first. Remembering the material is a lot easier when you know what it means. Trying to do accounting by rote does not work.

Take notes. Listening is extremely important. A recent study indicates that most people retain only ten to fifteen percent of what they hear within 72 hours. Since you need to remember this information for several weeks, if not years, you must write it down. This same study shows that your retention rate increases dramatically when you see something rather than hear it. If you use the information (do the assignments, understand the concepts) the retention rate shoots up to 85 percent. Notetaking is essential, but you must learn to take notes efficiently, accurately, and quickly, so that you don't jeopardize your ability to listen effectively.

Make a friend. Exchange telephone numbers with at least one person in the class. Call this person when you need to find out about classwork you have missed and assignments or notes that are incomplete or unclear.

Be prepared. Before going to class, preview the material to be covered and make sure assignments due are completed and familiar to you. Often students spend hours completing an assignment ahead of time only to arrive in class not remembering how they achieved their results. Make a list of questions you have regarding new material, then during the class check off these questions as they are explained. If the lesson does not answer all your questions, be sure to ask the questions that remain.

Refer to the math aids. Your text contains a chapter called Mathematical Presentations (Appendix A), which will give you an idea of the type of math required for your accounting course. In addition, this booklet contains a Math Review explaining the simple math that we need for accounting, but that many of us have not used since grade school. You may also want to ask your instructor what other aids are available for a general review of math.

CLASSWORK: THE OPTIONS

These are things you may *choose* to do. You should only attempt one or two of the following suggestions at any one time. If you decide a particular one does not work for you, try a different one. It is important for you to try some of these, but don't try them all at once. That would be not only impossible, but thoroughly unnecessary.

If the professor consents, tape record the class and transcribe the material later. This has two advantages. First, when you are not concerned with taking notes you are able to actively listen much more effectively. Second, the process of transcribing the material gives you another opportunity to hear the lesson.

Keep a class journal. After each class, take the time to write down what you did in class that day and any questions, problems, or general observations about the material or the class itself. If you did have questions, see if you can find the answers in your reading or in the next class. If not, list the questions and make a point of finding the answers before too much time expires. Remember, accounting is a cumulative process, and if you don't understand now, you may not be able to understand later.

Summarize. At the end of each class, take a few minutes to write a summary of what was discussed and taught during the class. Unlike a class journal, the summary should contain only factual information about the course work. Review your summary to verify that it is accurate and complete. Later these summaries will provide an invaluable study tool.

Outline. At the end of each class, prepare an outline of the key points covered. Keep all the outlines together in chronological order. Over a period of time these outlines should clarify the objectives of the course and provide you with a quick review of all topics covered.

Practice listening. Have a friend or relative relate a story or explain something to you. Either write down or tell the person what you heard. You should be able to relate all the major points if you have understood and remembered all that was said. Many of us believe we are more effective listeners than we actually are. Remember when you played "telephone" as a child?

Periodically exchange class notes. Compare notes with a classmate to see whether you have the same understanding of important concepts and procedures. Does it appear that you have been attending the same lectures? If not, consider whether you need to change your notetaking methods, or whether you can make constructive suggestions to your classmate.

HOMEWORK AND STUDY HABITS: THE ESSENTIALS

These are things you *must* do in order to learn the material and do well in your accounting course.

Read the assigned chapter in the text carefully. Study the exhibits and summary problems in detail, and make sure that you understand the math calculations illustrated. Write down any questions you have and find the answers.

Relate the chapter to real life. Most people have experience with earning money, paying taxes, taking loans, and other matters that relate to accounting. Try to find connections between the accounting topics you are learning and your own experiences and personal finances.

Attempt the assigned homework prior to attending class. Read the requirements and the information provided carefully. Look back over the chapter to see if you can find a similar problem illustrated. Even if you can't complete the assignment, at least you will be familiar with the material when the professor reviews it. Write down why you were unable to complete it, and what you did not understand. Sometimes just writing out your problem clarifies what you are confused about and what you need to go back over in order to find the solution.

When working on exercises and problems in the text, refer to the description given next to the assignment number. This will identify the topic being addressed, and will guide you back to the proper section in the chapter when necessary.

Keep up with the work. Waiting until the last minute does not give you the opportunity to digest, interpret and reflect upon the material. You need time to see relationships and connections between the material and concepts. Allow yourself enough time to complete the assignment. If you have trouble with the work, take a break. Quite often taking a break gives you a fresh outlook on the problem. Something that seems impossible may become obvious when you come back to it or look at it from a different perspective.

Find out what resources are available to you. Resources that are available with your text include the *Study Guide* with demonstration and practice problems; the *Prentice Hall Accounting Tapes*, a series of twenty videos each presenting a half-hour study of an individual text chapter; and *Making It Count*, a computerized tutorial that enables you to solve problems using the software included. In addition, your instructor may assign one of the many practice sets both in manual and computerized form. Within the text itself there are additional resources such as vocabulary lists, a glossary, self-study questions, chapter questions, end-of-chapter summaries, decision problems, and financial statement problems. Some of these items may be assigned by your professor, but they are also available to you individually to enhance the learning process. At many schools, tutoring and/or resource centers (labs) are offered. Make a point to find out if these are available to you, and take advantage of them. Not all schools will have all the resources listed, and not all will be necessary for you. You must investigate which ones are available and then decide which are most appropriate for you to use.

Arrive at your classroom a few minutes early. Use this time to review the material or discuss assignments and course material with your classmates.

Be patient. In the early stages, accounting is like a puzzle. With a little time and effort, the pieces begin to fit. Don't be surprised if it takes a little time for this to happen.

When studying for a quiz or an exam:

- Reread all your classnotes, identify all those areas that you don't recall or that you need additional information on, and go back to the text to find the answers.

- Review all assignments completed for the exercises and problems applicable to the test, and then re-solve them *without* referring to the solutions, or do the alternate problems provided by your text. Quite often the answers will be familiar to you, but you may not remember the process used for solving the problems. You must be able to solve the problems without flipping back to the text.

When taking a quiz or exam:

- Do not cram! Staying up late or all night just before the test will result in your being exhausted, anxious, and unable to think clearly. You may even fall asleep and miss the test entirely!

- Arrive prepared. Make sure you bring pencils, pens, erasers, a calculator (if allowed), and any other materials you will require.

- When the test is distributed, look it over and quickly determine your strategy for taking it. Consider that you have an overall time limit, that you may work more efficiently by solving the problems you know best first, that you must limit the amount of time you spend on each problem, and that some problems will have a higher point value than others.

- Relax. Do not let the time limit or the language used destroy your confidence. Take a few deep breaths, write any notes or formulas you've memorized down on the back of the test, and read the instructions carefully. Do not do more work than is required, and do not allow yourself to get bogged down in looking for errors. Very often students get so upset over trying to make a particular form balance that they run out of time to complete the remaining problems. Points lost for not balancing are minimal, but omitting a problem reduces the grade drastically. When errors occur, go on to the rest of the test, and return later to look for the error, if time permits.

HOMEWORK AND STUDY HABITS: THE OPTIONS

These are things you may choose to do. You should attempt only a few of the following suggestions at any one time. If you decide a particular one does not work for you, try a different one. It is important for you to try to do some of these, but don't try to do them all at once. This would be not only impossible but thoroughly unnecessary.

Review first.   Before you begin to work on an assignment, read the requirements given for it, then review in detail the applicable summary problem presented in the chapter.   There are usually two summary problems in each chapter, and one of these should help you understand the requirements of the assignment.   In addition, you may find the *Study Guide* demonstration problems useful because they are patterned after the summary problems, and the solutions provide step-by-step explanations.   The computerized tutorial, *Making It Count*, guides you through similar problems with frequent hints and a glossary window.

Define new words and terms.   If you encounter any difficulty with the wording of the assignment, use either the vocabulary list at the end of the chapter or the glossary at the back of the text to define unfamiliar terms.   Once you have done this, try rephrasing the problem using synonyms or language more familiar to you.   Keep a dictionary handy to look up words and terms not found in the glossary, and to check your spelling.   Keep a list of words that give you trouble to use as a handy reference.

Outline the key points in the assigned reading material.   Include page references in this outline in order to make it easy to look back when you require further detail.   Refer to the outline as you work on an exercise or problem.   When reading a chapter in the text, make sure you read the learning objectives provided at the beginning of the chapter first.   Note when each of these objectives is introduced.   You will find the objective in the margin at that point.   After reading that section, ask yourself if the objective has been satisfied and if you have understood it.   If not, make a list of questions you need to answer regarding this objective, and find the answers by re-reading the material, asking a classmate or the professor, or using other resources available to you.   The video lecture on the chapter may well answer most, if not all, of your questions.

Check into other sources.   Find additional articles or essays written on the same topic or relating to it.   As you read about a specific concept in accounting, try to find an example of it in a current newspaper or magazine article, or obtain a current annual report from a company and attempt to identify the terms and concepts that were discussed in the current chapter.   You can also use the published financial statement in Appendix C at the back of your text for this purpose.

Make comparisons and observations.   Study the current topic carefully. Determine the principles and concepts involved, observe the process required.   Compare the current topic you are working on to ones that you learned in the past.   Note similarities and differences.   Determine if the same concepts are used and/or applied consistently.   As you learn the steps in the accounting cycle, determine where each new topic fits in.

Make up a double entry journal.   When reading the chapter, divide your notebook page in half and label one side Notes and Quotes and the other Responses and Comments.   As you read, copy down (under Notes and Quotes) any items, definitions, terms, principles, concepts, and so on, that you feel are important. At the same time, use the other half of the page (Responses and Comments) to jot down any questions, references, comparisons, observations, thoughts, or ideas you have regarding the material. When you go back to study the chapter later, you have a ready reference to remind you of your earlier reading. An alternative is to do this in abbreviated form. As you read the chapter, underline or highlight the items you would have listed in Notes and Quotes, and use the wide margins the publisher has provided to write in your Responses and Comments.

Make predictions.   To enhance your interest, try to predict what you will read about next. For example, if you are reading about income and expense, you could predict that you will learn about profit next. Or if you are reading about buying an asset, you could predict that you will learn about selling an asset next. See how often your predictions are correct.

Form a study group.   Collaborate. Work with a friend or a group on an individual assignment or on a regular basis. Work together or "divide and conquer" the material. Not only can a study group make the work more palatable, but also there are proven benefits to group work. These include an increase in the collective and individual creativity of the group members, an improvement in critical thinking and communication skills, and increased self-confidence. During group work you learn how others think, react, agree, disagree, and you learn the art of compromise. These communication skills are especially important in accounting. Accounting is an information system that relies on the ability to accept information and convey it to others. For the most part, students are encouraged to be competitive during their educational experience. However, the accounting profession relies heavily on collaboration, on working closely with others in order to accomplish a particular objective. Communication skills and the ability to communicate effectively with co-workers, managers, clients, and other third parties becomes extremely important. A perfect way to get practice in communicating is by working within a group.   Be careful, though; the idea of working together is to have *all* participants provide input and support for one another. Pairs or groups do not work when one person does all the work or is expected to teach everyone else. Choose your partners carefully. Don't be afraid to "fire" group members who are not fulfilling their commitments.

Consider the time commitment of this course carefully.   The mastery of accounting takes time. Consider whether the number of hours you work or the number of credits you carry interferes with your ability to succeed in this course. Try to adjust your workload accordingly. Current studies indicate that full-time students (whether they are taking accounting or not) should not work more than twenty hours a week. If you need to work more hours, consider reducing your credit load. Keep in mind the end result, rather than the immediate objective.

Before an exam or a quiz:

- Answer the self study questions at the end of each chapter. Check your answers and find out why you made errors, if you did.

- Read the end-of-chapter summary. If it contains anything that you are unsure of or uncomfortable about, re-read the applicable sections of the chapter.

- On your own, answer the end-of-chapter questions that apply to the topics emphasized by your instructor. These provide additional review to complement the self-study questions.

- If you belong to study group, together try to develop or find examples of the problems you expect to see on the test. Work them out together or individually and then grade them. Note where you need additional study time.

- You may want to see how you do on a practice test. The *Study Guide* contains a substantial self-test for each chapter of the text. The *Study Guide* also provides a review of every objective covered in the chapter.

MATH REVIEW

INTRODUCTION

Many students come to the principles of accounting course with a background of trigonometry and calculus. Others have been out in the business world or have been caring for families. Most have not needed to apply simple arithmetic in an academic setting since elementary school.

The basics of accounting require, to a large degree, the application of practical mathematics. This math review is for students who want to refresh their memory and pick up a few tips for getting the math right.

ESTIMATING

See if you can identify with this recent experience of mine. I asked my class, "If the tax rate is 25%, and your income for the year is $80,000, what is your tax expense for the year?" All the calculators started to click, and one student called out, "$200,000." Another volunteered, "$320,000." Now taxes may be high, but the government does not normally expect taxpayers to contribute more than they earn. Why would intelligent students, working with calculators, produce answers that are obviously erroneous? There are two reasons.

The first reason is that they made common errors with their calculators. The first student misplaced the decimal. Instead of pressing $80,000 x .25 or $80,000 x 25%, this student pressed $80,000 x 2.5 and got an answer of $200,000. The other student used the wrong function key. Instead of pressing $80,000 x .25, this student pressed $80,000 ÷ .25 and got an answer of $320,000.

The second reason, and by far the more significant, is that these students *believed* what their calculators told them. Had they taken a moment to estimate what the answer should be, they would have recognized that their calculators were giving them improbable numbers.

Using the Calculator

We often think of calculators as infallible. It is true that if the calculator is working properly, it will give you a correct answer *based on the data that you input*. Wrong answers are almost always the result of faulty input. Faulty input may occur in several ways.

- *Wrong number.* First, you can input a wrong number. This often occurs repeatedly even if you clear the display and try the calculation again.
- *Wrong decimal.* Second, you can enter the numbers with the decimal point in the wrong place. This frequently occurs when you use the function of the calculator that sets the decimal point at two places for addition. When you have to multiply, divide, or take a percentage, the preset decimal no longer applies.
- *Wrong order.* Third, you can enter the numbers in incorrect order. The calculation 200 ÷ 500 (200 divided by 500) is often mistakenly entered as 500 ÷ 200 (200 divided into 500).
- *Wrong function.* Finally, you can press an improper function key. Pressing minus instead of plus, or divide instead of multiply, obviously will give a distorted answer.

How can you protect yourself against error, improve the quality of your work, and rely on the answers your calculator gives? *Estimate* your answer.

Using Estimates

Every calculation can be estimated with minimum effort by following these three steps:

1. Round your numbers to simplify the calculation. For example, you could round 11.215% to 10%. The degree of error is unimportant because the number is only an estimate.
2. Decide whether the answer (product, sum, difference, or quotient) should be larger or smaller than its components. It is surprising how often this elementary step prevents error.
3. If you are performing a series of calculations, check each one individually to see if the answer is reasonable. For, example, you should approach .22 x 8,050 + 1,960 as 20% or 1/5 of 8,000 (= 1,600), and then add 2,000. Your estimated answer is 3,600; the result of the actual calculation is 3,731. If you had made any of the four typical errors that we discussed, you most likely

would have seen a much larger difference between the answer on your calculator and your estimate.

If the answer on your calculator differs widely from your estimate, try the calculation again.

Now let's see how to estimate the amount of tax to pay on $80,000 of income taxed at 25%. First, the amount of tax has to be smaller than the amount of income. Second, 25% or 1/4 of 80 is 20, so .25 x $80,000 = $20,000. In this case, the estimate is also the exact calculation. My students could have worked the problem correctly in moments if only they had not relied on their calculators to the exclusion of common sense.

ROUNDING

You probably learned rounding in the elementary grades with one rule: If the number to be rounded is 5 or higher, round up, and if the number is less than 5, round down. What your teacher didn't tell you is that rounding will have a compound effect on subsequent computations.

Many of my students produce inaccurate results because of the compound effect of premature rounding. Premature rounding is rounding the number before you consider what effect it will have on subsequent computations. For example, when asked, "What is one-third of 8,700,000 dollars?" many students round the decimal that expresses 1/3 to .33. Then they multiply $8,700,000 by .33 and get $2,871,000 as an answer. However, if you divide $8,700,000 by 3, you get $2,900,000. That's a discrepancy of $29,000. What accounts for the discrepancy? The decimal .33, while close enough to a full third to give us a useful answer if we were working with small numbers, is not close enough to a full third to give us a useful answer when we work with large numbers.

What are the guidelines for accurate rounding?

Number of Decimal Places

First, ask yourself, "What will this number be used for later?" If you are going to multiply the resulting rounded number by a four-place number (1,000 - 9,999), then carry the rounded number out to four decimal places. If you are going to multiply the number by a six-place number (100,000 - 999,999), then carry the rounded number out to six decimal places, and so forth. You should also apply this rule when the rounded number will be involved in subsequent division.

Let's look again at our example, 1/3 of $8,700,000. The number 8,700,000 is a seven-place number, so the decimal for 1/3 should be carried out to seven places: $8,700,000 x .3333333. This calculation gives us $2,899,999.70—an error of only thirty cents (2,900,000 - 2,899,999.70 = $.30). Compare this result with the $29,000 error that occurred when $8,700,000 was multiplied by .33.

Chain Calculations

Next, ask yourself, "Do I need to round?" If the answer is yes, then ask yourself, "Can I use chain calculations or fractions instead?" When using the calculator, students often tend not to see the efficiency of chain calculations. Here is an example: To calculate (47,000 x 1/3) x 1,600, students often multiply 47,000 x 1/3, clear the screen and reenter the product into the calculator, and then multiply by 1,600. Not only is this method more time-consuming than making a chain calculation, but also it increases the chance of entering a wrong number.

Whenever possible, do *chain calculations*. To get an accurate answer to our example, we would:

1. enter 47,000 into the calculator
2. consider that 47,000 is a five-place number, and 1,600 is a four-place number; therefore, we should multiply by a decimal carried out to at least nine digits: 47,000 x .333333333
3. multiply by 1,600 without re-entering the prior product from Step 2

The result would be 47,000 x .333333333 = [15,666.66665] x 1,600 = 25,066,666.64.

Fractions

Accuracy can be significantly increased by using fractions instead of converted rounded decimals. In the preceding example, we could have divided 47,000 by 3 to get one-third, and multiplied the resulting number by 1,600: 47,000 ÷ 3 = [15,666.6666] x 1,600 = $25,066,666.65.

PERCENTAGES AND RATIOS

Another skill that many students have not exercised since grade school, but that becomes increasingly significant as you continue to learn accounting, is the ability to calculate percentages and ratios.

Percentages and ratios represent a proportion of a whole, just as fractions and decimals do. Fractions, decimals, percentages, and ratios all show the relationship between a part and the whole, and all can be expressed in terms of one another. For example, to express the relationship of one part to a whole consisting of four parts, we could use the fraction *1/4*, the decimal *.25*, the percentage *25%*, or the ratio *1:4*.

REMINDER: **To convert a fraction to a decimal, divide the numerator (the top number) by the denominator (the bottom number). To convert the**

decimal to a percentage, move the decimal point two places to the right and add a percent sign.

$$1/4 = 1 \div 4 = .25 = 25\%$$

Let's look at two common situations that require an understanding of proportion—a group purchase and a departmental cost.

Group Purchase

Companies often purchase several assets for one price. In order to keep proper accounting records, the companies must assign an appropriate value to each individual asset.

Suppose that a company buys at auction a group of three assets, and pays $80,000. Appraisers set a value of $50,000 on asset A, 30,000 on asset B, and $20,000 on asset C, which gives a total appraised value of $100,000. How much of the actual price of $80,000 should be assigned to each asset? We approach this problem from the standpoint that the sum of the parts equals the whole.

The first step is to divide the appraised value of each asset by the total appraised value (the parts as a proportion of the whole) to get a rate or percentage.

ASSET	APPRAISALS	EACH ASSET IS WHAT PART OF THE TOTAL APPRAISAL?
A	$ 50,000	$50,000/$100,000 = .50 or 5/10 or 50%*
B	30,000	$30,000/$100,000 = .30 or 3/10 or 30%*
C	20,000	$20,000/$100,000 = .20 or 2/10 or 20%*
	$100,000 total appraisal	

* The ratio of the parts to the whole could be expressed as 5:3:2.

The next step is to multiply each of the resulting proportions (expressed here as decimals) by the *actual* cost, $80,000.

ASSET	PROPORTION OF TOTAL APPRAISAL		ACTUAL COST OF 3 ASSETS		ALLOCATED VALUE EACH
A	.50	x	$80,000	=	$40,000
B	.30	x	80,000	=	24,000
C	.20	x	80,000	=	16,000
			$80,000 total cost		

The sum of the allocated values ($40,000, $24,000, and $16,000) equals the whole cost ($80,000).

Departmental Cost

Companies with more than one department must divide, or allocate, expenses fairly among their departments in order to keep useful accounting records.

Suppose that a company pays $40,000 a year to rent 5,000 square feet of space. Department X occupies 2,000 square feet of the space, and department Y occupies 3,000 square feet. How much of the $40,000 rent should be allocated to department X, and how much to department Y? Again, remember that the sum of the parts equals the whole.

Department X, with 2,000 out of 5,000 square feet, is occupying 2/5 of the total space and should be allocated 2/5 of the rent, or rent in the ratio of 2:5, or .40 times the rent, or 40% of the rent:

Department X: 2/5 x $40,000 = $16,000 or .40 x $40,000 = $16,000

Department Y, with 3,000 out of 5,000 square feet, is occupying 3/5 of the total space and should be allocated 3/5 of the rent, or rent in the ratio of 3:5, or .60 times the rent, or 60% of the rent:

Department Y: 3/5 x $40,000 = $24,000 or .60 x $40,000 = $24,000

Again, the sum of the allocated parts ($16,000 and $24,000) equals the whole ($40,000).

Uses in Accounting

A glance at your textbook will indicate a few of the contexts in which accountants use percentages and ratios. Assigning asset costs in group purchases is covered in Chapter 10. Allocating costs among departments is covered in Chapter 25. Chapter 8 describes the percentage of sales method of estimating bad debts. Chapter 12 demonstrates the percentage of completion method of recognizing revenue. Chapter 19 presents ratios that business people commonly use to compare net income and other significant figures when making investment and lending decisions. Chapter 26 uses the rate of return ratio to determine the advisability of buying a desired asset.

Other Uses of Math Techniques

The techniques of estimating, rounding, and calculating percentages will serve you well in other courses—finance, economics, statistics, and many more. In addition, you will find these techniques invaluable in your personal life—for balancing a checkbook, computing your income taxes, buying a car—whenever quantitative information is involved.

 **Additional Notes:**

 **Additional Notes:**

Additional Notes:

Additional Notes:

Additional Notes:

 **Additional Notes:**

**Additional Notes:**

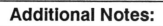**Additional Notes:**

 **Additional Notes:**